WHALE WADD

Written by Judith Fitzgerald
Illustrated by Maureen Paxton

© Judith Fitzgerald, 1986
© illustrations, Maureen Paxton, 1986

Published by Black Moss Press, P.O. Box 143, Station A, Windsor, Ontario, Canada. Financial assistance toward publication of this book was provided by the Canada Council and the Ontario Arts Council.

Black Moss Press books are distributed by Firefly Books, 3520 Pharmacy Ave., Unit 1-C, Scarborough, Ontario.

Printed and bound in Canada by Ampersand, Guelph, Ontario.

ISBN 0-88753-146-6

First printing January 1986

For

Meagan Allison-Hancock,
Jenna Berger and
Malcolm Sutherland

Whale Waddleby was as big as a boat —
He looked like a house in an overcoat.

And Whale Waddleby was the meanest bully
Who had ever lived in Bottlesea Gully.

Whale Waddleby was as mean as could be —
He wouldn't like you and he didn't like me.

The meaner Whale got, the bigger Whale grew —
He didn't like me and he wouldn't like you.

Whale Waddleby was so big, fat and mean,
He was the meanest mean you've ever seen.

Whale Waddleby wore the funniest shoes —
They were as huge as huge canoes.

His hat was as big as a submarine —
It was the biggest hat you've ever seen.

A floppy tent was Whale Waddleby's coat,
And it made him look like a walking boat.

And when Whale Waddleby walked downtown,
His footsteps thundered for miles around.

His footsteps thundered down each street,
And the pavement cracked beneath his feet.

Each morning Whale would roll out of bed,
Then he'd eat and eat until his face turned red.

He'd grumble and groan and gretch and gribble,
Then he'd drubble and drone and drooble and dribble.

Then he'd brush his teeth with old gasoline;
They were the meanest teeth you've ever seen.

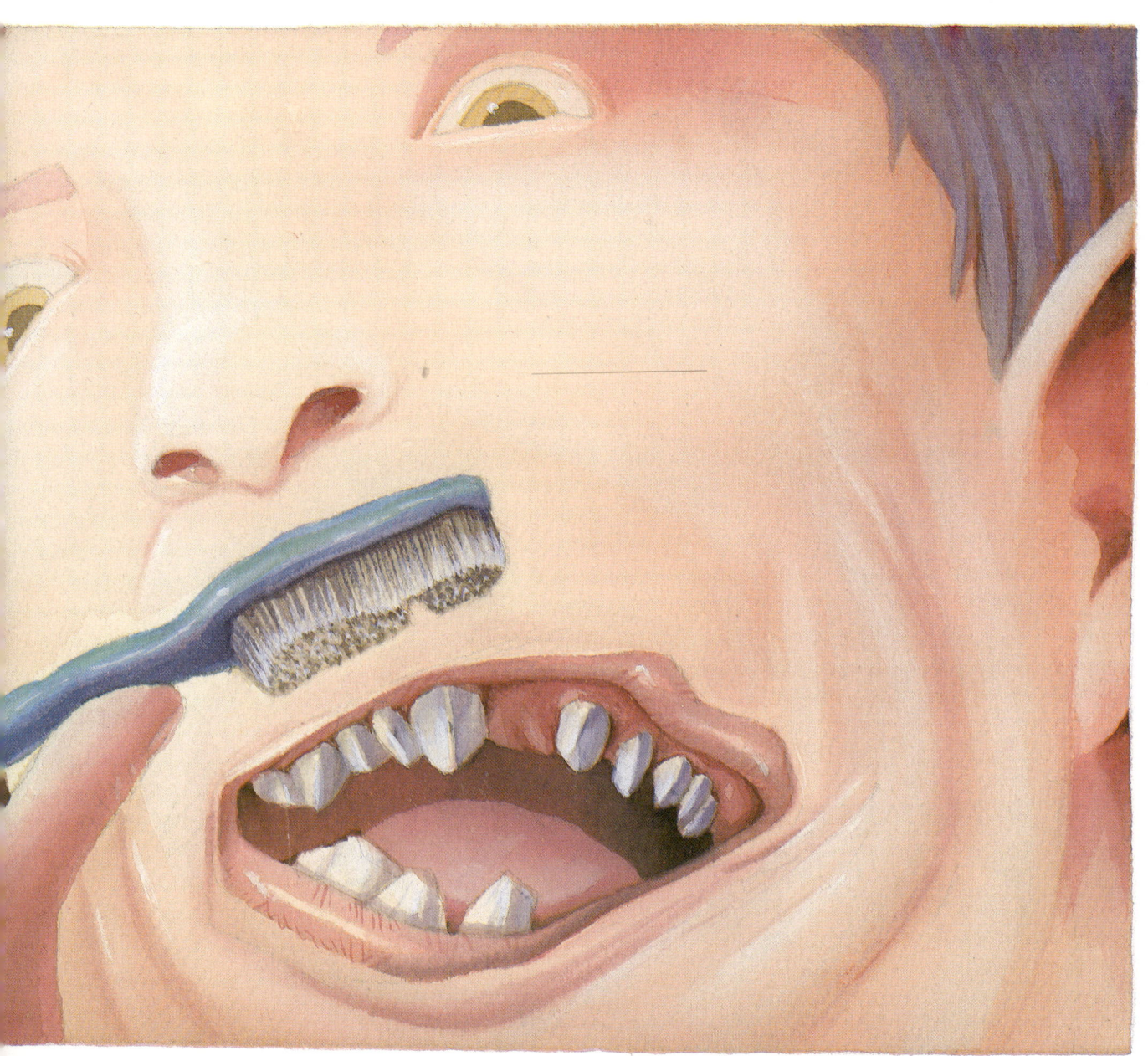

Then he'd crumble and rumble and tumble outside —
And cats would howl and dogs would hide.

Whale Waddleby laughed a laugh so mean:
"I'm the meanest bully you've ever seen!"

So the meanest bully you've even seen
Decided to slurp up some ice cream.

He widdled and waddled and woodled downtown;
He really looked like an oversized clown.

When he finally got to the ice cream store,
He niggled and noodled and niggled some more.

He snuffled and laughed and roffled and giggled —
His big nose waggled and his big ears wiggled.

All of a sudden Whale's big eyes popped,
His sniggling and fliggling suddenly stopped.

Whale Waddleby flopped down in the street,
And cracked the pavement beneath his seat.

In the window of the ice cream store,
The sign said, "CLOSED: GONE TO BORNASPORE."

"WHAT?" roared Whale, "YOU CAN'T DO THAT!"
He kicked off his shoes and tore off his hat.

He rangled and ringled and roggled and rolled,
The sun went down and Whale grew cold.

He ran up and down each Bottlesea street,
And each sidewalk broke beneath his feet.

He ran into every house and store,
Each sign said, "CLOSED: GONE TO BORNASPORE."

Whale Waddleby roared and rinkled and roaned,
He screamed and sckrinkled and scraped and groaned.

The houses were empty, the streets were bare;
Whale Waddleby was alone, there was no one there.

And the last we heard of the Bottlesea bully,
He was bullying himself in Bottlesea Gully.